KWANZAA: HOW TO CELEBRA

by Kathleen Minnick-Taylor
with illustrations by Charles Taylor II

This book contains all the information you need to celebrate Kwanzaa.

KWANZAA
Published by ROAR Enterprises, Inc.
P.O. Box 259869
Madison, WI 53725

ACKNOWLEDGEMENTS:
Camilla Rucinski, Chuck Taylor

BOOK DESIGN:
Elizabeth Johanna

KWANZAA KINARA CANDLES ON TITLE PAGE:
OCAL

DEDICATION

We dedicate this book to our son, Kemet. We love you! Mother and Father — Kathleen Minnick-Taylor and Charles Taylor.

SPECIAL THANKS

A special thanks to our extended family members and friends who posed for many of the illustrations used in this book.

EXPLANATION OF SPELLING

Except for African American, Afri<u>k</u>a and Afri<u>k</u>an are spelled with a <u>k</u> throughout this book. Please see the Glossary for an explanation.

ISBN 0-935483-69-1

KWANZAA: HOW TO CELEBRATE IT IN YOUR HOME

WHAT IS KWANZAA?

KWANZAA (KWAHN-zah) is a seven-day African American cultural holiday, observed by peoples of Afrikan descent world-wide. It is a joyous celebration to reaffirm traditional Afrikan social values. It is therefore non-religious and non-heroic. The word **"KWANZAA"** is derived from a Swahili phrase, **"MATUNDA YA KWANZA"** (mah-TOON-dah yah KWAHN-zah), meaning "first fruits." In Afrika, harvesting the first fruits or crops of the season was cause for celebration. The African American version of **KWANZAA** was inspired by the traditional Afrikan ritual celebrating the harvest of the first fruits. An extra "a" was added to the ending of the word KWANZAA todistinguish the African American celebration.

WHEN WAS IT FOUNDED AND BY WHOM?

KWANZAA was created by university professor and cultural scholar Dr. Maulana Karenga in 1966. His vision has resulted in one of the most important holidays observed by African Americans in the United States.

WHEN IS KWANZAA CELEBRATED?

The annual seven-day ritual begins the day after Christmas, December 26, and ends on New Year's Day — January 1.

WHY IS IT IMPORTANT TO CELEBRATE KWANZAA?

KWANZAA is meant to foster a reunion of African American families and peoples, to recognize African American achievements, and to be a time for cultural renewal and rededication to strong family values.

HOW DO WE CELEBRATE KWANZAA?

KWANZAA begins and ends with a **TAMSHI LA TAMBIKO** (TAHM-shee lah-tam-BEE-ko), a libation statement of hope and encouragement. **KWANZAA** is filled with symbolism, Swahili words, and a daily candle-lighting ritual. Each day a different **KWANZAA** principle is celebrated. The principles are the guide-posts of the celebration. The meaning of each principle is discussed, and a family activity is planned around it. In our home, we wear Afrikan clothing, add music, affirmations and the **KWANZAA** pledge to our daily ritual. We greet each other with the Swahili greeting, **"HABARI GANI"** (hah-BAR-ree GAH-nee), meaning, "what's the news?" We respond with the principle for that day.

On the following pages, we have provided "how-to" information on our family and our extended family's daily ritual. Our main celebration occurs around supper time. We encourage you to use our ritual as a guide for celebrating **KWANZAA** in your home. Keep in mind that while the principles and symbols of **KWANZAA** remain the same, you should feel free to modify our ritual to fit your circumstances. **KWANZAA YENU IWE NA HERI!** (KWAHN-zah yeh-noo ee-weh nah her-ree), "may your Kwanzaa be happy!"

Preparing the harvest of the first fruits — **KWANZAA**

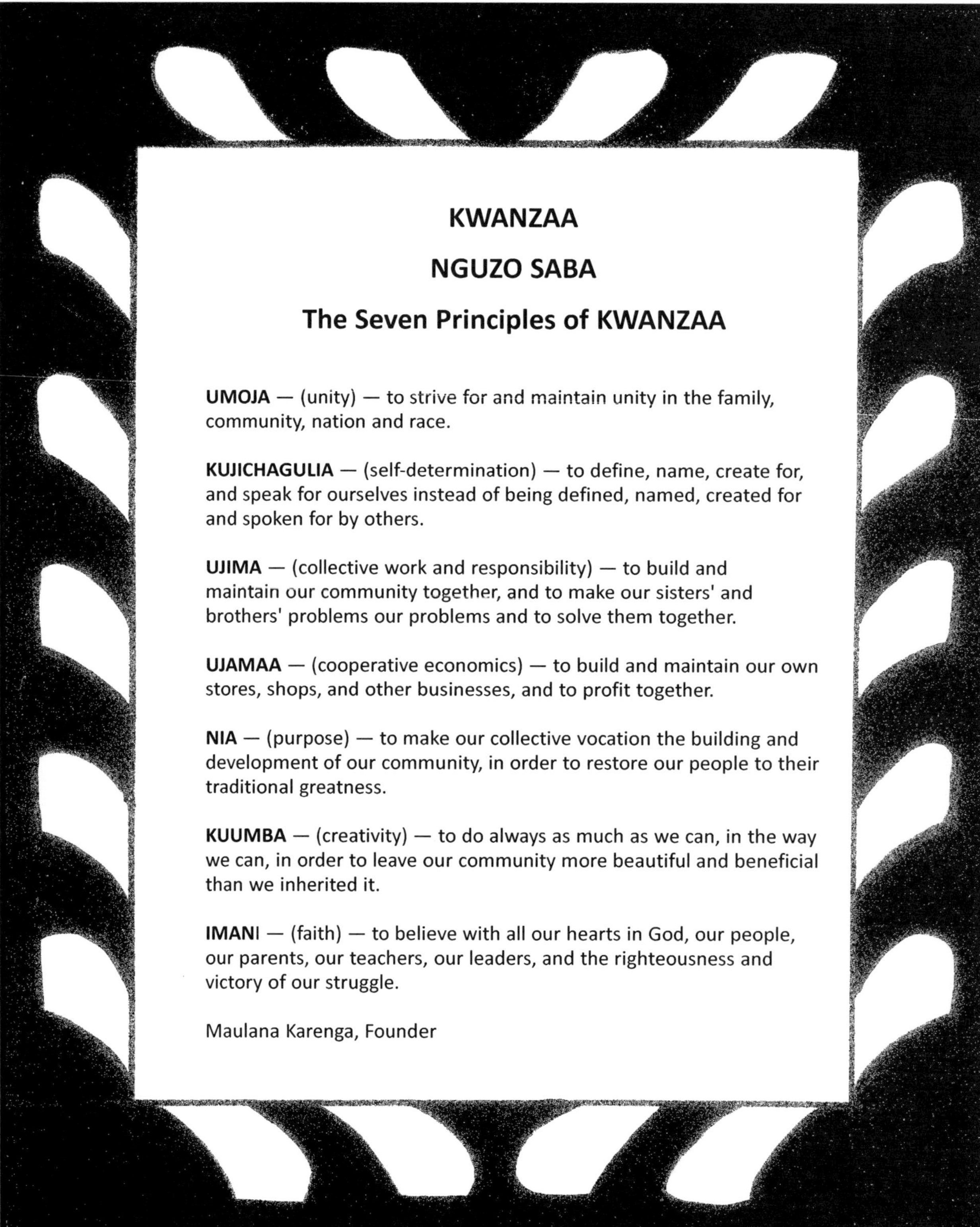

KWANZAA

NGUZO SABA

The Seven Principles of KWANZAA

UMOJA — (unity) — to strive for and maintain unity in the family, community, nation and race.

KUJICHAGULIA — (self-determination) — to define, name, create for, and speak for ourselves instead of being defined, named, created for and spoken for by others.

UJIMA — (collective work and responsibility) — to build and maintain our community together, and to make our sisters' and brothers' problems our problems and to solve them together.

UJAMAA — (cooperative economics) — to build and maintain our own stores, shops, and other businesses, and to profit together.

NIA — (purpose) — to make our collective vocation the building and development of our community, in order to restore our people to their traditional greatness.

KUUMBA — (creativity) — to do always as much as we can, in the way we can, in order to leave our community more beautiful and beneficial than we inherited it.

IMANI — (faith) — to believe with all our hearts in God, our people, our parents, our teachers, our leaders, and the righteousness and victory of our struggle.

Maulana Karenga, Founder

HOW DO WE PREPARE OUR HOME FOR KWANZAA?

Prior to the celebration, decorate one or more rooms in your home with red, black and green items. These are the colors of **KWANZAA. RED** symbolizes the blood that has been shed by Afrikan people in their quest for freedom. **BLACK** represents the color and culture of Afrikan people and **GREEN** symbolizes the land of our roots—Mother Afrika—and the promise of a better future.

In our home, we adorn the family room with Afrikan beads, Afrikan art, and kinte cloth, along with the **KWANZAA** display. We've found these preparations add a festive flare to our **KWANZAA** celebration.

WHAT CULTURAL SYMBOLS ARE NEEDED TO CELEBRATE KWANZAA AND WHAT ARE THEIR MEANINGS?

A **MKEKA** (mm-KAY-kah), a mat, is used to represent Afrikan traditions, symbolizing the foundation on which all else rests.

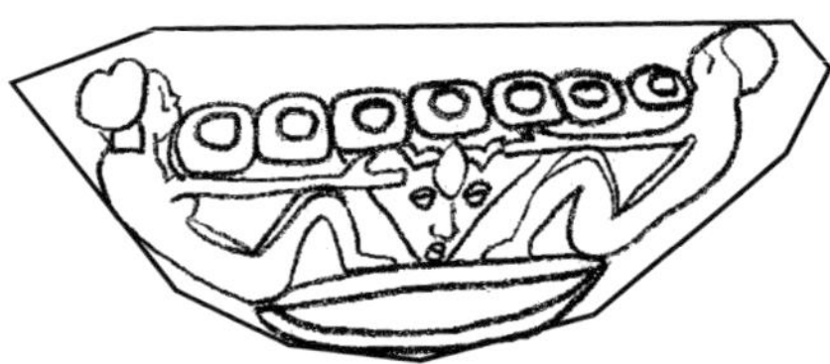

The **KINARA** (kee-NAH-rah), a candleholder, represents the original stalk of our ancestry.

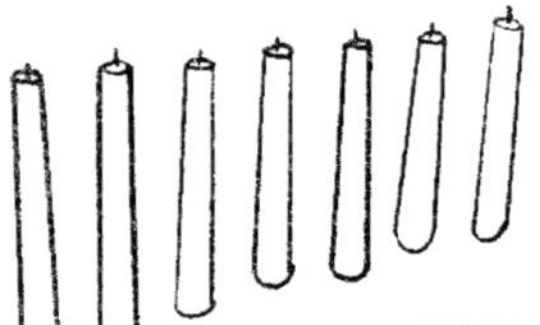

MISHUMAA SABA (mee-SHOO-mah SAH-ba), seven candles, are placed in the KINARA. Three are red, three are green and one is black, representing **NGUZO SABA** (nn-GOO-zoh SAH-bah), the seven principles, on which Kwanzaa is based. In the ceremony, the black candle is always lit first to represent the present, followed by red representing the past and green which represents the future of Afrikan people.

VIBUNZI (vee-BOON-zee), ears of corn, represent the number of children in a family. If you don't have children, corn can still be used to represent yourself as your parents' child.

KIKOMBE CHA UMOJA (kee-KOOM-bay cha oo-MOH-jah), a communal unity cup, is used in the ceremony to share the drink. This act of passing and drinking from the unity cup, depicts unity among Afrikan people.

MAZAO (mah-ZAH-oo), crops, fruits and vegetables, are symbolic of products generated from hard work and labor throughout the year.

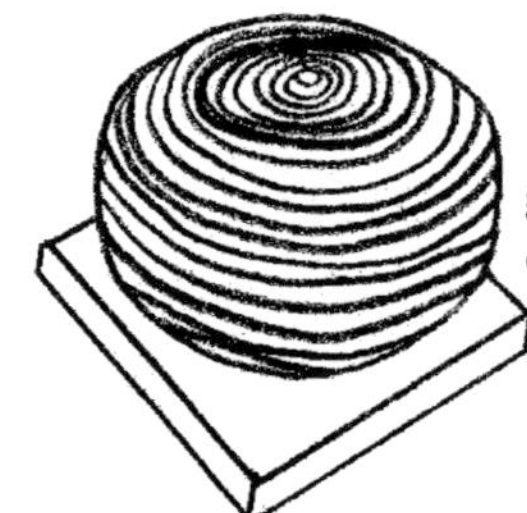

ZAWADI (zaa-WAH-dee), gifts, represent rewards for outstanding achievement in applying the **NGUZO SABA** during the year.

In addition to the seven symbols above, our family includes the **BENDERA YA TAIFA** (tri-color flag) and a framed copy of the **NGUZO SABA** as part of the **KWANZAA** display.

HOW IS THE KWANZAA DISPLAY ARRANGED?

Place a **MKEKA** on a low table. Next, place the **KINARA** on the **MKEKA.** Arrange the three red and the three green **MISHUMAA SABA** to the far left and far right in the **KINARA.** Place the one black candle in the center of the **KINARA.** You can also hang a colorful poster or framed copy of the **KWANZAA** principles above the display. Then, place the **VIBUNZI** along the sides of the **KINARA,** and place the **KIKOMBE** near it, as well. Be sure to add an array of **MAZAO** on the table and stand the **BENDERA YA TAIFA** close to it. Last, a variety of **ZAWADI** can be placed around the table. You now have a complete and colorful **KWANZAA** display. If you are unable to obtain all of the **KWANZAA** cultural symbols, keep in mind that it is the **KWANZAA** principles that are most important.

CELEBRATING NGUZO SABA — THE SEVEN PRINCIPLES OF KWANZAA

OPENING LIBATION

After sprinkling drops of water from the unity cup in the directions of the four winds — north, south, east and west, to honor Afrikan people worldwide, the oldest among us begins the **KWANZAA** celebration with the **TAMSHI LA TAMBIKO** below:

As we begin this celebration let us pause to remember all who came before us and their great sacrifices. Let us honor the motherland Afrika, while pledging to lift America to a higher calling. During the next seven days let us renew our commitment to the KWANZAA principles, and let them renew in our hearts a belief in our people. **"HARAMBEE!"** Now we are ready to celebrate the first principle of **KWANZAA.**

HOW KWANZAA IS CELEBRATED

DAY 1 — DEC. 26

PRINCIPLE — UMOJA (oo-MOH-jah), meaning unity.

AFFIRMATION — "Unity within the family, community and race will uplift our spirits and preserve our cultural base."

RITUAL — During the day, we greet each other by saying, **"HABARI GANI."** We reply by saying, **"UMOJA."** Before we sit down for supper, we put on African American music to play softly in the background. Then we prepare to light the candle. Since this is the first day of the **KWANZAA** celebration, in honor of our elders, the eldest person in our extended family is asked to light the candle. Only one candle is lit on the first day–the black candle, symbolizing unity among Afrikan peoples.

After the candle is lit, we read the above affirmation in unison. Next we pass the unity cup, which we usually fill with water or juice. Beginning with the eldest person, each of us briefly tells what **UMOJA** means, takes a drink and then passes the cup until all have drunk. Lastly, we repeat the **KWANZAA** pledge in unison. We then sit down for supper. During supper we discuss what we have done to promote unity and what additional things we might do in the future.

After supper we engage in a family activity. For **UMOJA** we create a family picture board. We go through family pictures, talk about our family history, tell family stories about the pictures, note family resemblances, and then work together to assemble a picture board that will stay up the entire seven days of **KWANZAA.** Afterwards we form a circle and speak the Afrikan chant, **"HARAMBEE,"** once. We then blow out the candle, bringing an end to the celebration of the first principle — **UMOJA.** With our spirits filled, we eagerly anticipate rejoicing in the second principle tomorrow.

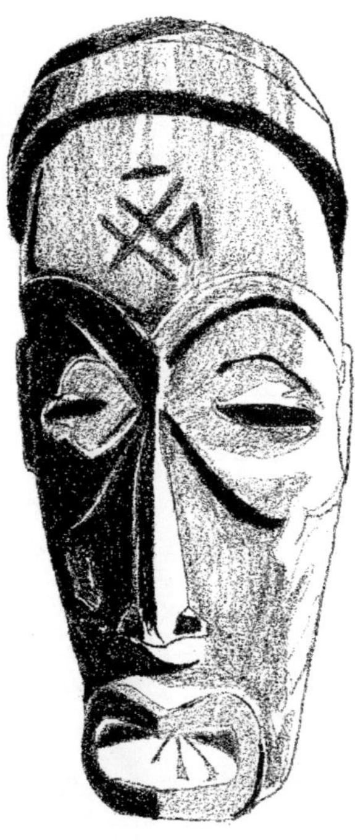

HOW KWANZAA IS CELEBRATED

DAY 2 — DEC. 27

PRINCIPLE — KUJICHAGULIA (koo-GEE-cha-GOO-lee-ah), meaning self-determination.

AFFIRMATION — "Define and create your own course in life. Remember, you are responsible for your actions and decisions."

RITUAL — During the day, when we are greeted with "HABARI GANI," we reply by saying, **"KUJICHAGULIA."** We follow the same ritual as before, except this night we light two candles, a black and a red one. The black candle is always lit first and then used to light the red candle. The red candle represents the second principle — self-determination. After the candles are lit, we read the above affirmation together. As we pass and drink from the filled unity cup, we each briefly share what **KUJICHAGULIA** means to us. Before sitting down for supper, we repeat the **KWANZAA** pledge.

During our meal, we discuss what we have done to apply self-determination and how we can continue this practice in the future. After supper, we write our family oath. We do this every year on this day to celebrate **KUJICHAGULIA.** The oath is read during the **KWANZAA KARAMU** festival. Last year we adopted the following oath: "Be mindful and kind to those around you, and be aware of how your actions affect others." After we write our oath, we ask the youngest among us to tack the oath on the family picture board. Our oath stays on the picture board until the **KWANZAA KARAMU** festival is over. To end the day we say, **"HARAMBEE, HARAMBEE,"** twice. We then blow out the candles, bringing an end to the celebration of **KUJICHAGULIA.**

HOW KWANZAA IS CELEBRATED

DAY 3 — DEC. 28

PRINCIPLE — UJIMA (oo-GEE-mah), meaning collective work and responsibility.

AFFIRMATION — "Working together leads to prosperity for our people."

RITUAL — Each time we are greeted with **"HABARI GANI,"** we reply by saying, **"UJIMA."** Before we sit down for supper, we follow the same ritual as before. On this night, we light three candles. A green candle is lit for **UJIMA** symbolizing the hope for our future work together. After the candles are lit we recite the above affirmation, in unison. As we pass the unity cup, we repeat the **KWANZAA** pledge. We gather around the supper table to discuss UJIMA further. After supper, we make plans for the **KWANZAA KARAMU** (kah-RAH-moo) a feast and festival held on the last day of **KWANZAA.** We plan the menu filled with family favorite recipes, review the invitation list, and decide on special readings and music. Children from our extended family make plans to present a special skit for the festival. They select a theme based on the principle of **UJIMA.** By the end of the evening, all plans are finalized. We hold hands and shout, **"HARAMBEE, HARAMBEE, HARAMBEE,"** three times. We then blow out the candles, bringing an end to the celebration of **UJIMA**. This evening reminds all of us of the joy and strength we gain by working together.

HOW KWANZAA IS CELEBRATED

DAY 4 — DEC. 29

PRINCIPLE — UJAMAA (oo-JAH-mah), meaning cooperative economics.

AFFIRMATION — "If I buy from you and you buy from me, we both will prosper."

RITUAL — We answer the **"HABARI GANI"** greeting by replying, **"UJAMAA."** On this day we engage in our family activity before the candle-lighting ceremony. Each month during the past year, we put our loose change in what we call the **KWANZAA** savings jar. On December 29, we take the money from the jar, shop at a black-owned business and buy a book for a child in our extended family. We ask the child to study the book and perform a reading at the **KARAMU.** Later that evening we light four candles including a second red candle. As on other nights, the lighting of a red candle causes us to reflect on our past. As we share the unity cup we talk about the meaning of cooperative economics. Together we proudly state the above affirmation. As we sit down to supper our conversation is filled with creative ideas to better support growth within ourselves and within black owned businesses. After supper, we recite the **KWANZAA** pledge. We then hold hands and shout, **"HARAMBEE,"** four times. The candles are blown out, bringing an end to the celebration of **UJAMAA.**

HOW KWANZAA IS CELEBRATED

DAY 5 — DEC. 30

PRINCIPLE — NIA (NEE-ah), meaning purpose.

AFFIRMATION — "Our purpose in life is to help one another!"

RITUAL — When we hear the greeting **"HABARI GANI"** we answer by replying, **"NIA!"** Prior to our family supper we light five candles including a second green candle. As we say tonight's affirmation, we are reminded that the lighting of each green candle represents the hope for our future together. We tell ourselves that life's true meaning can be found inside each of us. Then we recite the **KWANZAA** pledge in unison. During supper, we discuss how we have applied **NIA** to our daily lives. After supper we turn off all the lights and meditate for a few minutes about our role in our family, our community, our nation, and our planet. After sharing our thoughts we hold hands and shout, **"HARAMBEE"** five times. We then blow out the candles ending the celebration of **NIA.**

HOW KWANZAA IS CELEBRATED

DAY 6 — DEC. 31

PRINCIPLE — KUUMBA (koo-OOM-bah), meaning creativity

AFFIRMATION — "We're only limited by our imagination, so we must always dream big."

RITUAL — We reply, **"KUUMBA"** each time we are greeted with **"HABARI GANI."** We light six candles, including the last red one, representing the six principles we've observed thus far. Together we read aloud the above affirmation. Tonight as we pass the unity cup, we reflect on our ancestral heritage and how our people have embraced **KUUMBA**. We then read the **KWANZAA** pledge, slowly and conscientiously, allowing time and room for reflection.

During supper we talk about goals we have accomplished during the last year and new dreams that we have for the coming one. Tonight we also excitedly plan special items we can make for the **KARAMU,** including simple gifts, drawings, table name cards, and festival banners. Lastly on this night, we always wrap books that will be given as rewards at the **KARAMU** in praise of the children's good works. We are now ready for the last day of **KWANZAA**. We take extra pleasure tonight in our gathering together, as we raise our fists upward and shout, **"HARAMBEE"** six times before blowing out the candles ending the celebration of **KUUMBA.**

HOW KWANZAA IS CELEBRATED

DAY 7 — JAN. 1

PRINCIPLE — IMANI (ee-MAH-nee), meaning faith

AFFIRMATION — "Let us develop a never-ending capacity for hope in our people."

RITUAL — We reply, **"IMANI,"** to the **"HABARI GANI"** greeting. This last day of celebration is truly a family affair at our house. We spend part of the morning planting a seed with the faith that it will come to life in the spring. We place the planted seed in the center of the **KWANZAA** display and then recite the above affirmation in unison. As evening approaches, we gather together in great anticipation. This is the night of the **KWANZAA KARAMU.** It is symbolic of celebrating the Afrikan harvest. We open our home to our relatives and close friends. Everyone brings a dish to pass and gifts to exchange. We try to make the occasion as joyous as possible. Prior to sitting down for the feast, we light all seven candles. We say the name of each principle as we light that candle. As we pass the unity cup we recite the **KWANZAA** pledge with one strong, sure voice. We place **KWANZAA** greeting cards at the dinner table with affirmations written on them. During the meal, each person is asked to read an affirmation. Over dessert, we each reflect on what **KWANZAA** has meant to us and how we plan to keep the principles alive throughout the new year.

KWANZAA KARAMU

After supper, the fun begins. The youngest child who is able to, reads our family oath. We have music, songs, readings, poetry and the special children's skit before we exchange gifts.

KWANZAA KARAMU

We dance and celebrate late into the night.

KWANZAA KARAMU

When the dancing ends, we all stand, form a circle and hold hands. We blow out one candle at a time and repeat the name of the principle the candle represents. Then the eldest person holds the unity cup skyward and repeats the closing libation to end the KWANZAA celebration.

KWANZAA CLOSING TAMSHI LA TAMBIKO

"As we conclude our annual **KWANZAA** celebration, let us remember that the true meaning of KWANZAA lies in its principles. If we strive to live these principles daily, we will not only have learned valuable lessons from our Afrikan past, we will have assumed responsibility for our future. You are each leaving with three powerful gifts which no one can take away from you. You have:

1) seven **KWANZAA** principles to keep you grounded and on course;

2) an inner light that was strengthened by the daily lighting of each candle; and

3) the knowledge and comfort that you are part of a family, community and people, so you will never, ever be alone.

So, go forward in faith and hope. Now give each other a communal embrace. Peace be with you. **HARAMBEE!"**

We repeat **"HARAMBEE, "** seven times, then hug one another and wish each other well, bringing an end to the **KWANZAA** celebration!

KWANZAA PLEDGE

We pledge to be:

Keepers of our culture
Wise in our decisions
Active in our communities
Noble to our elders
Zealous in our efforts for progress
Advocates for our children
Achievers in all of our endeavors

HARAMBEE! (hah-RAHM-bay)
– meaning, "Let's Pull Together!"

BENDERA YA TAIFA (ben-DER-ah yah tah-EE-fah) is the tri-color flag used in the KWANZAA celebration, created by Marcus Garvey, founder of the Universal Negro Improvement Association.

GLOSSARY OF TERMS

Afrika and Afrikan — spelled with a k because as author Haki R. Madhubuti says, "Africa is not the true name of that continent. Therefore the k represents a redefined Afrika."

Bendera (ben-DER-ah) — the red, black and green flag designed by Marcus Garvey and adopted for use in the Kwanzaa celebration by Dr. Maulana Karenga, the founder of Kwanzaa.

Habari Gani (hah-BAR-ree GAH-nee) — Swahili phrase, "What is the news?"

Harambee (hah-RAHM-bay) — a continental Afrikan chant, "Let's pull together."

Imani (ee-MAH-nee) — the seventh principle of Kwanzaa, meaning faith.

Karamu (kah-RAH-moo) — feast.

Kikombe (kee-KOOM-bay) — a unity cup used in the Kwanzaa celebration to share the drink.

Kinara (kee-NAH-rah) — a seven-spaced candleholder used during the Kwanzaa celebration.

Kujichagulia (koo-GEE-cha-GOO-lee-ah) — the second Kwanzaa principle, self-determination.

Kuumba (koo-OOM-bah) — the sixth Kwanzaa principle, creativity.

Kwanzaa Yenu Iwe Na Heri (KWAHN-zah yeh-noo ee-weh nah heh-ree) — "may your Kwanzaa be happy."

Matunda Ya Kwanza (mah-TOON-dah yah KWAHN-zah) — first fruits of the harvest.

Mazao (mah-ZAH-oo) — crops, the fruits and vegetables that represent the reward for hard work and labor throughout the year.

Mkeka (mm-KAY-kah) — a straw mat used in the Kwanzaa display.

Mishumaa Saba (mee-SHOO-ma SAH-bah) — seven candles; three are red, three are green and one is black. They are placed in the Kinara and represent the seven principles (Nguzo Saba) of Kwanzaa.

Nguzo Saba (nn-GOO-zoh SAH-ba) — the seven principles of Kwanzaa.

Nia (NEE-ah) — the fifth Kwanzaa principle, purpose.

Tamshi La Tambiko (TAHM-shee lah tam-BEE-ko) — libation statement.

Ujamaa (oo-JAH-mah) — The fourth principle of Kwanzaa, cooperative economics.

Ujima (oo-GEE-mah) — the third Kwanzaa principle, collective work and responsibility.

GLOSSARY OF TERMS Continued

Umoja (oo-MOH-jah) — the first Kwanzaa principle, unity.

Vibunzi (vee-BOON-ZEE) — ears of corn, representing the number of children in a family.

Zawadi (zaa-WAH-dee) — gifts given at the end of the Kwanzaa celebration.

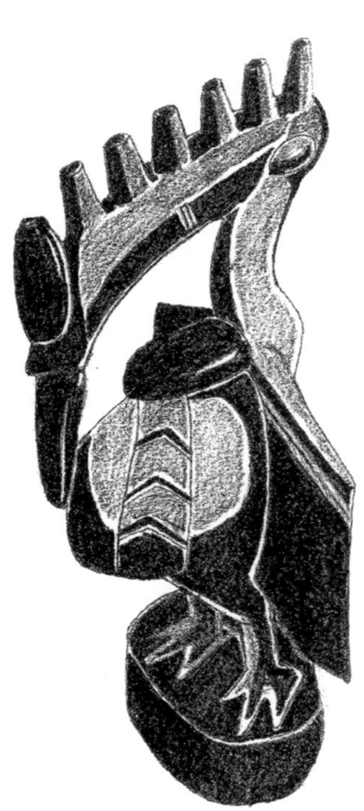

REFERENCES

Karenga, Maulana. ***KWANZAA: A Celebration of Family, Community and Culture.*** Los Angeles: University of Sankore Press, 2008.

Morninghouse, Sundaira. ***HABARI GANI? What's the News?: A KWANZAA Story***. Seattle: Open Hand Publishing, Inc., 1992.

Pinkney, Andrea Davis. ***Seven Candles for KWANZAA.*** New York: Dial Books for Young Readers, 1993.

Shealy, Valerie J.R Banks. ***KWANZAA, December 26-January 1: An Afrikan Celebration.*** Los Angeles: Sala Enterprises, 1991.

Official Kwanzaa website: http://www.officialkwanzaawebsite.org/index.shtml

Daily Candle Lighting Ceremony

When To Light

Black — then Red — then Green
(present) (past) (future)

Remember to always light the black candle first

ABOUT THE AUTHOR AND ILLUSTRATOR

Husband and wife team, Charles Taylor II and Kathleen Minnick-Taylor collaborated on this, their first book.

Kathleen Minnick- Taylor, a native of Louisiana, is a magna cum laude graduate of Grambling State University. She attended graduate school at the University of Wisconsin-Madison. Reading nonfiction, creative writing and listening to jazz are her hobbies.

Charles Taylor II is a native of Missouri. He majored in studio arts at Kent State University in Kent, Ohio. He is currently a computer programmer and App designer. Reading Afrikan history and computer coding are his passions.

"After explaining and sharing our version of celebrating Kwanzaa with you, we hope you understand the principles of Kwanzaa as a cultural celebration and tribute to self-development. We encourage you to apply the NGUZO SABA daily, because these guidelines provide inspiration for self-enrichment, enlightenment and encouragement. Happy KWANZAA!"

-KMT & CT

86229268R00015

Made in the USA
Columbia, SC
28 December 2017